TAB

MW01289571

INTRODUCTION

Accounting principles provide a standard that can be used no matter what organisation. Imagine if there were no common standards and everybody involved in undertaking accounting followed their own system, or no system at all, this would make it extremely difficult or possibly you would not know whether or not a corporation was profitable or not. Most corporations follow what are known as General Accepted Accounting Principles (GAAP) and there is vast space set aside in libraries and bookstores devoted to just this one topic. Unless an organization states otherwise, anyone reading a monetary statement usually will assume that the corporation concerned has used GAAP. As with any assumptions, do not fully rely on them, ask the questions to give yourself clarity.

If GAAP principles are not being used for preparing a corporations financial statements, then the corporation needs to create a clear statement that a different kind of accounting method is being used and they are bound to avoid using titles in their monetary statements that would mislead the person examining it, that they are using GAAP. In fact they should advise what accounting principles they are using.

GAAP is the highest standard for preparing financial statements. A company that does not disclose that it has used principles as an alternative than GAAP makes a corporation legally responsible for any misleading or misunderstood data. These principles have been fine-tuned over decades and have effectively governed accounting ways and the monetary reporting systems of businesses. Totally different principles are established for different sorts of business entities, such for-profit and not-for-profit companies, governments and different enterprises.

However, GAAP is not a cut and dried, rigidly endorsed set of principles. GAAP is a series of pointers and as such are usually open to interpretation. Estimates may have been made at times due to insufficient data, but as a rule strict compliance on accuracy should be followed. You would have surely heard the phrase "creative accounting" and this can be when a corporation pushes the envelope a little (or a lot) to form their business look additional profitable than it may actually be. This is often also called massaging the numbers. This can get out of control and quickly flip into accounting fraud, which is also referred to as cooking the books. The results of those practices will be devastating and have ruined a lot of lives, as has been demonstrated in some of the large corporate failures.

If you ever wanted to know what is accounting then this is your change to learn? Who is in charge of setting basic accounting standards that we all follow? Is there some type of regulatory system is place to investigate and arrest people for accounting fraud? Well guess what, there is, at least to a certain degree any way. So here is a quick accounting principles education that can explain everything. Continue reading

WHAT IS ACCOUNTING? LEARN BASIC ACCOUNTING PRINCIPLES

First, just what is accounting anyway? Well in simple terms accounting is the comprehensive system of gathering and recording financial information of a business for the purpose of preparing summaries for tax authorizing, investors, managers and other who make decisions within the companies or organizations that they are involved in. The accounting terminology or terms can get tricky at times and you may need to keep handy an accounting glossary that explains the terms in plain language if you are a beginner. To keep people from ethics frauds in accounting the United States top experts created the Financial Accounting Standards Board or (FASB) for short. This was established in 1973 and it replaced the Accounting Principles Board (APB). The job of the (FASB) is to analyze and review problems in the field that is brought to them. After much deliberation they will make an assessment of what type of action that will be taken when an accounting issue occurs.

This was mainly voluntary and it had very good success. Double-entry accounting was founded in Italy in the 1400's and the accounting formula has change since then. The reason why the basic accounting concepts worked or well was that the business community would not be able to function properly if there were no consistency in the reporting of finances.The FASB has its' own private financing and is not government organized. The American Institute of Certified Public Accountants(AICPA) are a big supporter of the FASB and many of our Certified Public Accountants(CPAs) are members of this prestigious organization. Accounting careers are shaped on you being a member. They are bound by the guidelines and principles that they offer as other countries also have similar boards that require a high level of accounting conduct.

The FASB created the basic accounting concepts code known as General Accepted Accounting Principles (GAAP). The idea behind this is if everyone uses the same business financial statement prepared according to GAAP, then who ever uses the information can trust or rely on the information more steadily than if prepare differently. Any business that prepare their statements without using the GAAP standards, like a lot of small businesses do, cannot say that their statements are created under GAAP guidelines and they should let the user know they are not and let the buyer beware.

To keep a watch out on everything the government relies on the Securities Exchange Commission(SEC) to sort of police the accounting world. They mostly focus on public companies because they are responsible for protecting investors from fraudulent misrepresentation. The SEC has established it own set of accounting standards and with the economy the way it is today they really have their hands full with this.

Accountants are now more involved with preparing income tax returns and they use their business financial statements. The Internal Revenue Service(IRS) may review those financial records when they perform an audit and not following the rules can get you into big trouble risking fines and penalties.

As you can see the principles and standards in many ways are a combination of voluntary and regulatory guidelines. There is a push to create an international accounting standards board or (IASB) due to the growing globalization process. This will be a huge undertaking that will surely take years to build. Now that the stock markets around the world are in trouble it is obviously needed.

TYPES OF ACCOUNTING

As a result of economic, industrial, and technological developments, different specialized fields in accounting have emerged.

The famous branches or types of accounting include: auditing, taxation, AIS, fiduciary, financial accounting, managerial accounting, cost accounting, and forensic accounting.

Forensic accounting

This field involves the reconstruction of financial information when a complete set of financial records is not available. This skill set can be used to reconstruct the records of a destroyed business, to reconstruct fraudulent records, to convert cash-basis accounting records to the accrual basis, and so forth. This career tends to attract auditors. It is usually a consulting position, since few businesses require the services of a full-time forensic accountant. Those in this field are more likely to be involved in the insurance industry, legal support, or within a specialty practice of an audit firm.

Management accounting

This field is concerned with the process of accumulating accounting information for internal operational reporting. It includes such areas as cost accounting and target costing. A career track in this area can eventually lead to the controller position, or can diverge into a number of specialty positions, such as cost accountant, billing clerk, payables clerk, and payroll clerk.

Financial accounting

This field is concerned with the aggregation of financial information into external reports. Financial accounting requires detailed knowledge of the accounting framework used by the reader of a company's financial statements, such as Generally Accepted Accounting Principles (GAAP) or International Financial Reporting Standards (IFRS). Or, if a company is publicly-held, it requires a knowledge of the standards issued by the government entity responsible for public company reporting in a specific country (such as the Securities and Exchange Commission in the United States). There are several career tracks involved in financial accounting. There is a specialty in external reporting, which usually involves a detailed knowledge of accounting standards. There is also the controller track, which requires a combined knowledge of financial and management accounting.

Public accounting.

This field investigates the financial statements and supporting accounting systems of client companies, to provide assurance that the financial statements assembled by clients fairly present their financial results and financial position. This field requires excellent knowledge of the relevant accounting framework, as well as an inquiring personality that can delve into client systems as needed. The career track here is to progress through various audit staff positions to become an audit partner.

Fiduciary Accounting

Fiduciary accounting involves handling of accounts managed by a person entrusted with the custody and management of property of or for the benefit of another person. Examples of fiduciary accounting include trust accounting, receivership, and estate accounting.

Government accounting

This field uses a unique accounting framework to create and manage funds, from which cash is disbursed to pay for a number of expenditures related to the provision of services by a government entity. Government accounting requires such a different skill set that accountants tend to specialize within this area for their entire careers.

Cost Accounting

Sometimes considered as a subset of management accounting, cost accounting refers to the recording, presentation, and analysis of manufacturing costs. Cost accounting is very useful in manufacturing businesses since they have the most complicated costing process.

Cost accountants also analyze actual and standard costs

to help managers determine future courses of action regarding the company's operations.

Tax accounting

This field is concerned with the proper compliance with tax regulations, tax filings, and tax planning to reduce a company's tax burden in the future. There are multiple tax specialties, tracking toward the tax manager position.

Internal auditing

This field is concerned with the examination of a company's systems and transactions to spot control weaknesses, fraud, waste, and mismanagement, and the reporting of these findings to management. The career track progresses from various internal auditor positions to the manager of internal audit. There are specialties available, such as the information systems auditor and the environmental auditor.

Accounting Information Systems

Accounting information systems (AIS) involves the development, installation, implementation, and monitoring of accounting procedures and systems used in the accounting process. It includes the employment of business forms, accounting personnel direction, and software management.

ELEMENTS OF ACCOUNTING: ASSETS, LIABILITIES, AND CAPITAL

The three major elements of accounting are: Assets, Liabilities, and Capital.

These terms are used widely in accounting so it is necessary that we take a close look at each element. But before we go into them, we need to understand what an "account" is first.

What is an Account?

The term "account" is a descriptive storage unit used to collect and store information of similar nature.

For example, "Cash".

Cash is an account that stores all transactions that involve cash receipts and cash payments. All cash receipts are recorded as increases in "Cash" and all payments are recorded as deductions in the same account.

Another example, "Building". Suppose a company acquires a building and pays in cash. That transaction would be recorded in the "Building" account for the acquisition of the building and a reduction in the "Cash" account for the payment made.

Now, let's take a look at the accounting elements.

Assets

Assets refer to resources owned and controlled by the entity as a result of past transactions and events, from which future economic benefits are expected to flow to the entity. In simple terms, assets are properties or rights owned by the business. They may be classified as current or non-current.

A. Current assets

Assets are considered current if they are held for the purpose of being traded, expected to be realized or consumed within twelve months after the end of the period or its normal operating cycle (whichever is longer), or if it is cash. Examples of current asset accounts are:

- Cash and Cash Equivalents – bills, coins, funds for current purposes, checks, cash in bank, etc.
- Receivables – Accounts Receivable (receivable from customers), Notes Receivable (receivables supported by promissory notes), Rent Receivable, Interest Receivable, Due from Employees (or Advances to Employees), and other claims

Allowance for Doubtful Accounts – This is a valuation account which shows the estimated uncollectible amount of accounts receivable. It is a contra-asset account and is presented as a deduction to the related asset – accounts receivable.

- Inventories – assets held for sale in the ordinary course of business
- Prepaid expenses – expenses paid in advance, such as, Prepaid Rent, Prepaid Insurance, Prepaid Advertising, and Office Supplies

B. Non-current assets

Assets that do not meet the criteria to be classified as current. Hence, they are long-term in nature – useful for a period longer that 12 months or the company's normal operating cycle. Examples of non-current asset accounts include:

- Long-term investments – investments for long-term purposes such as investment in stocks, bonds, and properties; and funds set up for long-term purposes
- Land – land area owned for business operations (not for sale)
- Building – such as office building, factory, warehouse, or store
- Equipment – Machinery, Furniture and Fixtures (shelves, tables, chairs, etc.), Office Equipment, Computer Equipment, Delivery Equipment, and others

Accumulated Depreciation – This is a valuation account which represents the decrease in value of a fixed asset due to continued use, wear & tear, passage of time, and obsolescence. It is a contra-asset account and is presented as a deduction to the related fixed asset.

- Intangibles – long-term assets with no physical substance, such as goodwill, patent, copyright, trademark, etc.
- Other long-term assets

Liabilities

Liabilities are economic obligations or payables of the business.

Company assets come from 2 major sources – borrowings from lenders or creditors, and contributions by the owners. The first refers to liabilities; the second to capital.

Liabilities represent claims by other parties aside from the owners against the assets of a company.

Like assets, liabilities may be classified as either current or non-current.

A. Current liabilities

A liability is considered current if it is due within 12

months after the end of the balance sheet date. In other words, they are expected to be paid in the next year.

If the company's normal operating cycle is longer than 12 months, a liability is considered current if it is due within the operating cycle.

Current liabilities include:

- Trade and other payables – such as Accounts Payable, Notes Payable, Interest Payable, Rent Payable, Accrued Expenses, etc.
- Current provisions – estimated short-term liabilities that are probable and can be measured reliably
- Short-term borrowings – financing arrangements, credit arrangements or loans that are short-term in nature
- Current-portion of a long-term liability – the portion of a long-term borrowing that is currently due.
- Example: For long-term loans that are to be paid in annual installments, the portion to be paid next year is considered current liability; the rest, non-current.
- Current tax liabilities – taxes for the period and are currently payable

B. Non-current liabilities

Liabilities are considered non-current if they are not

currently payable, i.e. they are not due within the next 12 months after the end of the accounting period or the company's normal operating cycle, whichever is shorter.

In other words, non-current liabilities are those that do not meet the criteria to be considered current. Hah! Make sense? Non-current liabilities include:

- Long-term notes, bonds, and mortgage payables;
- Deferred tax liabilities; and
- Other long-term obligations

Capital

Also known as net assets or equity, capital refers to what is left to the owners after all liabilities are settled. Simply stated, capital is equal to total assets minus total liabilities. Capital is affected by the following:

- Initial and additional contributions of owner/s (investments),
- Withdrawals made by owner/s (dividends for corporations),
- Income, and
- Expenses.

Owner contributions and income increase capital. Withdrawals and expenses decrease it.

The terms used to refer to a company's capital portion varies according to the form of ownership. In a sole proprietorship business, the capital is called Owner's Equity or Owner's Capital; in partnerships, it is called Partners' Equity or Partners' Capital; and in corporations, Stockholders' Equity.

In addition to the three elements mentioned above, there are two items that are also considered as key elements in accounting. They are income and expense. Nonetheless, these items are ultimately included as part of capital.

Income

Income refers to an increase in economic benefit during the accounting period in the form of an increase in asset or a decrease in liability that results in increase in equity, other than contribution from owners.

Income encompasses revenues and gains.

Revenues refer to the amounts earned from the company's ordinary course of business such as professional fees or service revenue for service companies and sales for merchandising and manufacturing concerns.

Gains come from other activities, such as gain on sale of equipment, gain on sale of short-term investments, and other gains.

Income is measured every period and is ultimately included in the capital account. Examples of income accounts are: Service Revenue, Professional Fees, Rent Income, Commission Income, Interest Income, Royalty Income, and Sales.

Expense

Expenses are decreases in economic benefit during the accounting period in the form of a decrease in asset or an increase in liability that result in decrease in equity, other than distribution to owners.

Expenses include ordinary expenses such as Cost of Sales, Advertising Expense, Rent Expense, Salaries Expense, Income Tax, Repairs Expense, etc.; and losses such as Loss from Fire, Typhoon Loss, and Loss from Theft. Like income, expenses are also measured every period and then closed as part of capital.

Net income refers to all income minus all expenses.

AREAS OF ACCOUNTING PRACTICE

Accounting career opportunities may be divided into four broad areas or scope of practice.

Government Accounting

Government agencies also need accountants. These agencies need accounting information to help them plan, budget, forecast, and allocate government funds. State auditors are also employed by the government to ensure the proper use and allocation of the said funds.

Accounting Education

This area is made up of accountants who are into teaching, research, and training & development. Accountants can pursue a career as a faculty member in a school, an author of an accounting book, a researcher, a trainer, or a reviewer.

Public Accounting

Accountants in public practice are working in accounting firms or individually to provide audit and attestation, tax planning and preparation, and advisory services to their clients.

Accountants in public accounting serve clients on a project or contractual basis.

In CPA firms, new accountants start as accounting or audit staff and work their way up to the junior accountant, senior accountant, supervisor, manager, and partner positions. After gaining enough experience, they may also start a public accounting firm of their own.

Private Accounting

In private accounting, also known as practice in commerce and industry, an accountant serves only one company. Accountants in private accounting provide a staff function which supports the company by performing accounting-related tasks.

Positions in private practice include entry-level jobs such as bookkeeper, accounting clerk, financial analyst, internal auditor, and others. From there, new entrants can work their way up the organizational chart and get to key management positions such as Chief Internal Auditor, Controller (Chief Management Accountant or Chief Accounting Officer), and Chief Financial Officer (CFO).

ACCOUNTING PRINCIPLES - THE REAL DEAL

If everyone committed in the process of line followed their own grouping, or no method at all, there's be no way to truly affirm whether a society was moneymaking or not. Most companies originate what are titled mostly acknowledged statement principles, or GAAP, and there are large tomes in libraries and bookstores devoted to right this one message. Unless a accompany states otherwise, anyone representation a financial evidence can attain the supposition that lot has used Aggregation.

If GAAP are not the principles victimized for preparing business statements, then a playing needs to kind trenchant which added grade of line they're misused and are confine to refrain using titles in its financial statements that could guide the organism examining it.

GAAP are the gold acceptable for preparing financial statement. Not disclosing that it has victimized principles additional than GAAP makes a organisation wrongfully liable for any misleading or misunderstood data. These principles bang been fine-tuned over decades and eff effectively governed occupation methods and the business reportage systems of businesses. Incompatible principles get been grooved for varied types of concern entities, much for-profit and not-for-profit companies, governments and otherwise enterprises.

Assemblage are not cut and dehydrated, still. They're guidelines and as specified are ofttimes lawless to reading. Estimates feature to be made at nowadays, and they enjoin nice institution efforts towards truth. You've sure heard the expression "generative occupation" and this is when a associate pushes the envelope a immature (or a lot) to head their line look author utile than it strength actually be. This is also called massaging the book. This can get out of suppress and apace work into job guile, which is also called cookery the books. The results of these practices can be devastating.

WHY ARE ACCOUNTING PRINCIPLES IMPORTANT?

Generally Accepted Accounting Principles are important because they set the rules for reporting and bookkeeping. These rules, often called the GAAP framework, maintain consistency in financial reporting from company to company across all industries.

Remember, the entire point of financial accounting is to provide useful information to financial statement users. If everyone reported their financial information differently, it would be difficult to compare companies. Accounting principles set the rules for reporting financial information, so all companies can be compared uniformly.

WHAT IS THE PURPOSE OF ACCOUNTING PRINCIPLES?

The purpose of accounting principles is to establish the framework for how financial accounting is recorded and reported on financial statements. When every company follows the same framework and rules, investors, creditors, and other financial statement users will have an easier time understanding the reports and making decisions based on them.

BASIC ACCOUNTING PRINCIPLES

A number of basic accounting principles have been developed through common usage. They form the basis upon which the complete suite of accounting standards have been built. The best-known of these principles are as follows:

Reliability principle

This is the concept that only those transactions that can be proven should be recorded. For example, a supplier invoice is solid evidence that an expense has been recorded. This concept is of prime interest to auditors, who are constantly in search of the evidence supporting transactions.

Revenue recognition principle

This is the concept that you should only recognize revenue when the business has substantially completed the earnings process. So many people have skirted around the fringes of this concept to commit reporting fraud that a variety of standard-setting bodies have developed a massive amount of information about what constitutes proper revenue recognition.

Consistency principle

This is the concept that, once you adopt an accounting principle or method, you should continue to use it until a demonstrably better principle or method comes along. Not following the consistency principle means that a business could continually jump between different accounting treatments of its transactions that makes its long-term financial results extremely difficult to discern.

Cost principle

This is the concept that a business should only record its assets, liabilities, and equity investments at their original purchase costs. This principle is becoming less valid, as a host of accounting standards are heading in the direction of adjusting assets and liabilities to their fair values.

Economic entity principle

This is the concept that the transactions of a business should be kept separate from those of its owners and other businesses. This prevents intermingling of assets and liabilities among multiple entities, which can cause considerable difficulties when the financial statements of a fledgling business are first audited.

Full disclosure principle

This is the concept that you should include in or alongside the financial statements of a business all of the information that may impact a reader's understanding of those statements. The accounting standards have greatly amplified upon this concept in specifying an enormous number of informational disclosures.

Time period principle

This is the concept that a business should report the results of its operations over a standard period of time. This may qualify as the most glaringly obvious of all accounting principles, but is intended to create a standard set of comparable periods, which is useful for trend analysis.

Accrual principle

This is the concept that accounting transactions should

be recorded in the accounting periods when they actually occur, rather than in the periods when there are cash flows associated with them. This is the foundation of the accrual basis of accounting. It is important for the construction of financial statements that show what actually happened in an accounting period, rather than being artificially delayed or accelerated by the associated cash flows. For example, if you ignored the accrual principle, you would record an expense only when you paid for it, which might incorporate a lengthy delay caused by the payment terms for the associated supplier invoice.

Conservatism principle

This is the concept that you should record expenses and liabilities as soon as possible, but to record revenues and assets only when you are sure that they will occur. This introduces a conservative slant to the financial statements that may yield lower reported profits, since revenue and asset recognition may be delayed for some time. Conversely, this principle tends to encourage the recordation of losses earlier, rather than later. This concept can be taken too far, where a business persistently misstates its results to be worse than is realistically the case.

Going concern principle

This is the concept that a business will remain in operation for the foreseeable future. This means that you would be justified in deferring the recognition of some expenses, such as depreciation, until later periods. Otherwise, you would have to recognize all expenses at once and not defer any of them.

Matching principle

This is the concept that, when you record revenue, you should record all related expenses at the same time. Thus, you charge inventory to the cost of goods sold at the same time that you record revenue from the sale of those inventory items. This is a cornerstone of the accrual basis of accounting. The cash basis of accounting does not use the matching the principle.

Monetary unit principle

This is the concept that a business should only record transactions that can be stated in terms of a unit of currency. Thus, it is easy enough to record the purchase of a fixed asset, since it was bought for a specific price, whereas the value of the quality control system of a business is not recorded. This concept keeps a business from engaging in an excessive level of estimation in deriving the value of its assets and liabilities.

Materiality principle

This is the concept that you should record a transaction in the accounting records if not doing so might have altered the decision making process of someone reading the company's financial statements. This is quite a vague concept that is difficult to quantify, which has led some of the more picayune controllers to record even the smallest transactions.

KEY ACCOUNTING ASSUMPTIONS

Here is a list of the key accounting assumptions that make up generally accepted accounting principles:

- Monetary Unit Assumption
- Periodicity Assumption

Monetary Unit Assumption

Monetary Unit Assumption – assumes that all financial transactions are recorded in a stable currency. This is essential for the usefulness of a financial report. Companies that record their financial activities in currencies experiencing hyper-inflation will distort the true financial picture of the company.

Periodicity Assumption

Periodicity Assumption – simply states that companies should be able to record their financial activities during a certain period of time. The standard time periods usually include a full year or quarter year.

FUNDAMENTAL ACCOUNTING CONCEPTS AND CONSTRAINTS

Here is a list of the four basic accounting concepts and constraints that make up the GAAP framework in the US.

- Going Concern Concept
- Business Entity Concept
- Industry Practices Constraint
- Materiality Concept

Going Concern Concept

Going Concern Concept – states that companies need to be treated as if they are going to continue to exist. This means that we must assume the company isn't going to be dissolved or declare bankruptcy unless we have evidence to the contrary. Thus, we should assume that there will be another accounting period in the future.

Business Entity Concept

Business Entity Concept – is the idea that the business and the owner of the business are separate entities and should be accounted for separately. This concept also applies to different businesses. Each business should account for its own transactions separately.

Industry Practices Constraint

Industry Practices Constraint – some industries have unique aspects about their business operation that don't conform to traditional accounting standards. Thus, companies in these industries are allowed to depart from GAAP for specific business events or transactions.

Materiality Concept

Materiality Concept – anything that would change a financial statement user's mind or decision about the company should be recorded or noted in the financial statements. If a business event occurred that is so insignificant that an investor or creditor wouldn't care about it, the event need not be recorded.

BENEFIT OF HAVING GOOD AND TIMELY FINANCIAL REPORT

While there are numerous benefits of having accurate and timely financial reports, we have identified few key benefits of financial statements.

Understanding the Financial Status of Your Business

The complete financial status of your business can be presented in a quality financial statement. The three main financial statements are the balance sheet, the income statement and the cash flow statement. The balance sheet reflects the owner's equity after the liabilities are subtracted from the assets. The income statement which is also known as the profit and loss statement shows the profit derived from income over a defined period of time.

A cash flow statement is a valuable tool for showing if there is enough cash coming in to pay for the operations of the business. A cash flow can be projected out over several months. The Income Statement shows how the restaurant and hotel perform over a period of time (i.e. a week, month or year). It takes all restaurant and hotel expenses into account, from prepaid expenses to expenses paid in the future. Overall, the Income Statement tells the operator if the business is making a profit. From there, the operator can begin making changes in policy and implementing strategies that will help the restaurant achieve its goals.

Should new sales programs be implemented? Does food cost in line with menu prices? Is the restaurant hitting its budgets? Can the owner(s) make distributions to the partners? These are some of the key questions that need to be addressed. The basic formula for an Income Statement is:

Sales - Cost of Goods Sold - Expenses = Profit/Loss

The Income Statement is everyone's favorite financial statement to review because it reveals the nature of the restaurants and hotel success. Restaurant and Hotel financial statements should be broken down into the following categories:

- Sales/room revenue
- Salaries
- Employee Benefits
- Controllable
- Occupancy
- General and Administrative
- Depreciation
- Interest
- Other Income

If sales and expenses are broken down into specific categories, the operator can easily compare and analyze his or her restaurant and hotel to industry standard percentages. Timely financial reporting will help to control the cost of goods sold like beverage cost food cost

The health of a restaurant and hotel can be analyzed from the Balance Sheet at any point in time (i.e. today, last month or tomorrow). The Balance Sheet allows operators to forecast short and long-term cash flow. As important as it is to review the Balance Sheet, few restaurants ever bother to prepare it. By checking the accuracy of the Balance Sheet, an operator can ensure the accuracy of the Income Statement. The Balance Sheet lists all the assets, liabilities and equity of the restaurant. The formula for the Balance Sheet is:

Assets = Liabilities + Equity

In the simplest terms, assets are what the business owns such as equipment, inventory or cash. Liabilities are what the business owes such as vendor bills, loans, notes, and leases. Even a gift certificate is a liability because the restaurant owes someone a meal at a future date. Equity is the ownership of the business.

It is important that assets and liabilities are properly classified on the Balance Sheet. To get a clearer picture of the business, an operator should break down the Balance Sheet into subcategories. The breakdown is explained as follows:

- Current Assets: assets with the life less than a year (i.e. cash, credit card receivables, inventory and prepaid expenses).

- Fixed Assets: assets with a life greater than a year that directly attributes to producing revenue (i.e. equipment, computers, furniture and leasehold improvements).
- Other Assets: assets with a life longer than a year that is not directly involved in the production of revenue (i.e. security deposits, trademarks and artwork).
- Liabilities require a similar classification and are broken down as follows:
- Current Liabilities: debts due within one year (i.e. accounts payable, accrued expenses, short-term loans and even gift certificates).
- Long-Term Liabilities: debts due that extend beyond one year (i.e. notes payable or long-term leases).

There is so much information to be gained from the Balance Sheet. For example, a restaurant and hoteliers that have large debts may have major cash flow problems. Identifying the current debts from the long-term debts on the Balance Sheet help determine the short and long-term cash needs, as well as the business potential success. Restaurateurs and hoteliers who take on large debts upon opening could be shooting themselves in the foot. The restaurant may show large profits based on the Income Statement, but the restaurant may not have money because it is paying out the outstanding debt (which is revealed in the Balance Sheet).

Most restaurants and hotels are set up as Partnerships or Sub Chapter S corporations, they have to explain all business expenses and income to all partner.

Better resource management

Due to timely frame financial report the restaurant owners and hoteliers will get accurate numbers of resources, therefore, they can use optimum use of all resources.

Sales Pattern

Financial statements reveal how much a restaurant owner and hoteliers earns per year in sales. The sales may fluctuate, but financial planners should be able to identify a pattern over years of sales figures. For example, the restaurant owner and hoteliers may have a pattern of increased sales when a new product is released. The sales may drop after a year or so of being on the market. This is beneficial, as it shows potential and sales patterns so executives know to expect a drop in sales.

Financial Statements Will Help Prepare A Budget And Make Financial Decisions

Timely financial reporting will help you prepare a budget and make an easy way to take the financial decisions to grow the business.

Performance Evaluation

Under this type of accounting practice, Business Owners may assess the performance of the Employees in the financial performance of the business.

Improved financial management

Timely financial reporting helps you to examine and correct any weaknesses in your financial systems. Improved financial management allows you to focus on current financial matters and develop future plans.

ACCOUNTING CONVENTIONS AND ACCOUNTING CONCEPTS

Relevance

The convention of relevance emphasizes the fact that only such information should be made available by accounting as is relevant and useful for achieving its objectives. For example, business is interested in knowing as to what has been total labor cost? It is not interested in knowing how much employees spend and what they save.

Feasibility

The convention of feasibility emphasizes that the time, labor and cost of analyzing accounting information should be compared vis-à-vis benefit arising out of it. For example, the cost of 'oiling and greasing' the machinery is so small that its break-up per unit produced will be meaningless and will amount to wastage of labor and time of the accounting staff.

Objectivity

The convention of objectivity emphasizes that accounting information should be measured and expressed by the standards which are commonly acceptable. For example, stock of goods lying unsold at the end of the year should be valued as its cost price not at a higher price even if it is likely to be sold at higher price in future. Reason is that no one can be sure about the price which will prevail in future.

Accounting Concepts

Materiality

It refers to the relative importance of an item or event. Those who make accounting decisions continually confront the need to make judgments regarding materiality. Is this item large enough for users of the information to be influenced by it? The essence of the materiality concept is : the omission or misstatement of an item is material if, in the light of surrounding circumstances, the magnitude of the item is such that it is probable that the judgment of a reasonable person relying on the report would have been changed or influenced by the inclusion or correction of the item.

Realization

This concept emphasizes that profit should be considered only when realized. The question is at what stage profit should be deemed to have accrued? Whether at the time of receiving the order or at the time of execution of the order or at the time of receiving the cash. For answering this question the accounting is in conformity with the law (Sales of Goods Act) and recognizes the principle of law i.e. the revenue is earned only when the goods are transferred. It means that profit is deemed to have accrued when 'property in goods passes to the buyer' viz. when sales are affected.

Matching

Though the business is a continuous affair yet its continuity is artificially split into several accounting years for determining its periodic results. This profit is the measure of the economic performance of a concern and as such it increases proprietor's equity. Since profit is an excess of revenue over expenditure it becomes necessary to bring together all revenues and expenses relating to the period under review. The realization and accrual concepts are essentially derived from the need of matching expenses with revenues earned during the accounting period. The earnings and expenses shown in an income statement must both refer to the same goods transferred or services rendered during the accounting period. The matching concept requires that expenses should be matched to the revenues of the appropriate accounting period. So we must determine the revenue earned during a particular accounting period and the expenses incurred to earn these revenues.

Accounting period

Though accounting practice believes in continuing entity concept i.e. life of the business is perpetual but still it has to report the 'results of the activity undertaken in specific period (normally one year). Thus accounting attempts to present the gains or losses earned or suffered by the business during the period under review. Normally, it is the calendar year (1st January to 31st December) but in other cases it may be financial year (1st April to 31st March) or any other period depending upon the convenience of the business or as per the business practices in country concerned.

Due to this concept it is necessary to take into account during the accounting period, all items of revenue and expenses accruing on the date of the accounting year. The problem confronting this concept is that proper allocation should be made between capital and revenue expenditure. Otherwise the results disclosed by the financial statements will be affected.

Entity

According to this concept, the task of measuring income and wealth is undertaken by accounting, for an identifiable Unit or Entity: The unit or entity so identified is treated different and distinct from its owners or contributors. In law the distinction between owners and the business is drawn only in the case of joint stock companies but in accounting this distinction is made in the case of sole proprietor and partnership firm as well. For example, goods used from the stock of the business for business purposes are treated as a business expenditure but similar goods used by the proprietor i.e. owner for his personal use are treated as his drawings. Such distinction between the owner and the business unit has helped accounting in reporting profitability more objectively and fairly. It has also led to the development of "responsibility accounting" which enables us to find out the profitability of even the different sub-units of the main business.

Stable Monetary Unit

Accounting presumes that the purchasing power of monetary unit, say Rupee, remains the same throughout. For example, the intrinsic worth of one Rupee is same and equal in the year 1,800 and 2,000 thus ignoring the effect of rising or falling purchasing power of monetary unit due to deflation or inflation. In spite of the fact that the assumption is unreal and the practice of ignoring changes in the value of money is now being extensively questioned, still the alternatives suggested to incorporate the changing value of money in accounting statements viz., current purchasing power method (CPP) and current cost accounting method (CCA) are in evolutionary stage. Therefore, for the time being we have to be content with the 'stable monetary unit' concept.

Conservatism

This concept emphasizes that profit should never be overstated or anticipated. Traditionally, accounting follows the rule "anticipate no profit and provide for all possible losses. For example, the closing stock is valued at cost price or market price, whichever is lower. The effect of the above is that in case market price has come down then provide for the 'anticipated loss' but if the market price has gone up then ignore the 'anticipated profits'.

Critics point out that conservation to an excess degree will result in the creation of secret reserve. This will be quite contrary to the doctrine of disclosure. However, conservatism to a reasonable degree may not come in for criticism.

Cost

This concept is closely related to the going concern concept. According to this, an asset is ordinarily recorded in the books at the price at which it was acquired i.e. at its cost price. This 'cost' serves the basis for the accounting of this asset during the subsequent period. This' cost' should not be confused with 'value'.

It must be remembered that as the real worth of the assets changes from time to time, it does not mean that the value of such an assets is wrongly recorded in the books. The book value of the assets as recorded do not reflect their real value. They do not signify that the values noted therein are the values for which they can be sold. Though the assets are recorded in the books at cost, in course of time, they become reduced in value on account of depreciation charges. In certain cases, only the assets like 'goodwill' when paid for will appear in the books at cost and when nothing is paid for, it will not appear even though this asset exists on name and fame created by a concern.

Therefore, the values attached to the assets in the balance sheet and the net income as shown in the Profit and Loss account cannot be said to reflect the correct measurement of the financial position of an undertaking, as they do not have any relation to the market value of the assets or their replacement values. This idea that the transactions should be recorded at cost rather than at a subjective or arbitrary value is known as Cost Concept. With the passage of time, the market value of fixed assets like land and buildings vary greatly from their cost.

These changes or variations in the value are generally ignored by the accountants and they continue to value them in the balance sheet at historical cost. The principle of valuing the fixed assets at their cost and not at market value is the underlying principle in cost concept. According to them, the current values alone will fairly represent the cost to the entity.

The cost principle is based on the principle of objectivity. The supporters of this method argue so long as the users of the financial statements have confidence in the statements, there is no necessity to change this method.

ACCOUNTING EQUATION

Dual concept may be stated as "for every debit, there is a credit." Every transaction should have two sided effect to the extent of same amount. This concept has resulted in Accounting Equation which states that at any point of time the assets of any entity must be equal (in monetary terms) to the total of owner's equity and outsider's liabilities. This may be expressed in the form of equation:

A-L = P

where

A stands for assets of the entity;

L stands for liabilities (outsider's claims) of the entity; and

P stands for Proprietor's claim (Capital) on the entity.

(The form of presentation of equation A-L = P is consistent with the legal interpretation of financial position. Thus it emphasizes that properly speaking the proprietary claim is the balance after providing for outsider's claims against the business from the total assets of the business).

INTRODUCTION TO FINANCIAL STATEMENTS: AN OVERVIEW

Financial statements refer to a specific set of reports produced in an entity's accounting system. The objective of these reports is to provide information about the entity.

A complete set of financial statements includes 5 components.

Statement of Comprehensive Income

The Income Statement, also known as Profit and Loss Statement (P&L Statement), shows the results of operations of an entity over a particular period of time. The income statement presents the period's income and expenses and the resulting net income or loss.

Many large companies today prepare a Statement of Comprehensive Income. The Statement of Comprehensive Income presents a company's results of operations (net income or loss) and its other comprehensive income (OCI). If the company has no other comprehensive income, then the contents of the Income Statement and Statement of Comprehensive Income would be the same.

Other comprehensive income include gains and losses that cannot be reported in the Income Statement such as revaluation surplus, translation adjustments, and unrealized gains, for a given period. Other comprehensive income is covered in higher financial accounting studies.

Statement of Financial Position

A Balance Sheet presents an entity's assets, liabilities, and capital as of a given point in time. This report shows the entity's financial position and condition, hence, also called Statement of Financial Position.

All asset amounts are added. All liability and capital accounts are also added. The total amount of assets should be equal to the total amount of liabilities plus capital.

Statement of Changes in Capital

The Statement of Changes in Capital (or Statement of Changes in Equity) shows the balance of the capital account at the beginning of the period, the changes that occurred during the period, and the ending balance as a result of such changes. Capital is affected by contributions and withdrawals of owners, income, and expenses.

The title used for this report varies depending upon the form of business ownership. It is called Statement of Owner's Equity in sole proprietorships, Statement of

Partners' Equity in partnerships and Statement of Stockholders' Equity in corporations.

Notes to Financial Statements

The Notes to Financial Statements, or Supplementary Notes, provide information in addition to those presented in the Balance Sheet, Income Statement, Statement of Changes in Equity, and Cash Flow Statement. The notes contain disclosures required by accounting standards, supporting computations, breakdown of line items in the face of the financial statements, and other information that users may be interested in.

Relationship among the Financial Statements

The financial statements contain interrelated information. This is the reason the financial statements are prepared in the sequence presented above. In fact, some of the figures in one financial statement component are actually taken from another component.

- The net income from the Income Statement is used in the Statement of Changes in Equity. Remember that income and expenses affect capital.
- The ending balance of capital in the Statement of Owner's/Partners'/SH's Equity is forwarded to the Balance Sheet (under Capital).
- The cash balance presented in the Balance Sheet

is supported by the Statement of Cash Flows. The ending balance of cash in the Statement of Cash Flows is the same amount presented in the Balance Sheet.

- The notes to financial statements show supporting computations of the amounts and additional information about the items presented in the above reports.

Statement of Cash Flows

The Statement of Cash Flows, or Cash Flow Statement, presents the beginning balance of cash, the changes that occurred during the period, and the cash balance at the end of the period as a result of the changes.

The cash flow statement shows the cash inflows and outflows from three activities: operating, investing, and financing.

Operating activities pertain to transactions that are directly related to the company's main course of business. Investing activities refer to "where the company puts its money". These activities include long-term investments, acquisition of property, plant and equipment; and other transactions related to non-current assets. Financing activities include transactions in which a company acquires its funds. These include loans from banks (long-term liabilities) and contributions from owners.

UNDERSTANDING OPERATING CASH FLOW

In this section, we're going to take a look at operating cash flow, which is one of the most important numbers in a company's accounts. Many investors pay a great deal of attention to these figures as it gives vital clues to an investor trying to assess the health, and value of a company.

What does Operating Cash Flow Means?

It's simply the amount of cash that company generates from its normal operations. For example, if you are a retailer like Walmart, the bulk of your revenue will come from the difference between the sale price of an item, and how much it costs you to sell it.

The operating cash flow shares a lot of similarities with E.B.I.T.D.A., that's earnings before interest taxes, depreciation, and amortization. And typically these numbers are not hugely different, that's why I say they're very similar.

The difference is due to working capital. I can assume you know what working capital is. One of the problems with learning accounting is that you have to learn multiple things at once. Eventually you will piece it all together.

Working Capital

So let's take a very quick look at working capital. Working capital is the difference between current assets and current liabilities. The word current simply means that it should be off the company's books within a year. So a current asset is something that is expected to be sold or consumed within one year.

Now, we can see the formula. Operating cash flow equals the net income plus non-cash expenses. This is typically depreciation and amortization, mainly let's add our power of E.B.I.T.DA., plus changes in working capital.

That's the fundamental formula for operating cash flow

Mathematically,

Working Capital = Current Assets - Current Liabilities = Net Income + Non-cash Expenses + Changes in Working Capital = FUNDAMENTAL FORMULA FOR OPERATING CASH FLOW.

Some Applications and How this is Useful to an Investor.

Working capital is very useful; the main use is that;

It can reveal dodgy accounting. For example; a company may generate huge profits but very little cash flow. This may indicate a problem, and you should be very skeptical about the source of the profit when it is not backed up by strong cash flows.

It gives you a more realistic idea of a company's health. Consider a retailer that owns its own stores, if the property market rockets, the company will report huge profits. But its flow of cash won't be huge. So when you go into those numbers, and analyze them, you'll see that the core business is not nearly as profitable as the overall profit figures would indicate. The other thing you need to be aware of is that

A company's cash flow is what is used to expand its business. So a company that is not generating much cash flow will need to get its expansion capital from somewhere else. Usually a bank.

Finally, now that you know what operating cash flow is, you can't just believe the statements figures. There are tricks that companies have used to make their numbers bigger. The classic one is extending the time taken to pay suppliers while collecting the money that's owed to you faster. You see how that would increase the operating numbers? Think of it. You're bringing in money faster and paying out slower. It's really a farce, but it gives the illusion of a higher operating numbers.

WAYS TO IMPROVE CASH FLOW

Do you operate a big retail-chain or a small service business?

If so, you'll already acknowledge how important regular cash flow is. Cash flow problems are often cited as the biggest reason why small, otherwise-profitable businesses, face problems.

So you need to get on top of it. Generating steady cash receipts is a key indicator of your success. If you rely on paying suppliers and service providers promptly, here are some tips to help improve your needs.

Cash Flow Analysis

If you're having trouble spotting patterns in your cash flow, carry out a detailed cash flow analysis. This will highlight where your cash is being generated and any future short-falls so you can tweak them.

For example, you may notice that your marketing advertising budget is consuming a large amount of your available cash. Knowing this will allow help you address any short-term needs, such as postponing payments.

Without analysing your cash requirements, it'll be harder for you to identify big gaps or determine the optimum solution to address your cash flow needs.

Allow subscription payments

Many small businesses generate regular cash receipts by offering customers opportunities to subscribe to specific services or purchases.

This method helps predict how much cash you'll have coming in from your subscribers. You can make more accurate forecasts and know how much spare cash you've got to work with.

Renegotiate payment times with suppliers

Many businesses struggle with larger suppliers' lead times and unhelpful payment time-frames. While you might not be able to convince all your suppliers to renegotiate terms, give it a try. By lengthening the time you need to pay, you'll give yourself extra breathing space, making things easier on your cash.

Don't purchase equipment upfront

While buying expensive equipment outright might save you money in the long-run, it could also harm your cash flow. Only make big purchases if you can really afford to do so. Otherwise, pay by instalments so that you can keep your cash flow in good order.

Consider leasing your equipment so that you retain more cash, which can be spent on day-to-day business operations and other important things.

Have a good credit line

While you won't want to rely on credit regularly, it can be super-useful to have a good credit line in place for emergencies. Get your credit sorted before you have a major shortfall, so you can keep your business running effectively.

Use direct debit

Consider setting up direct debit payment plans to help regulate your cash flow. They'll make it easier for clients to pay, and let you know exactly what you've got coming in and when.

So it's a win-win for your customers and you. Direct debit plans work especially well when used alongside an automated payment system. This can help you plan your cash needs and receive payments on time.

Virtual bookkeeping service

If your customers continually pay late, you could run out of cash. To receive payments faster, consider using a virtual bookkeeping service. These organisations often save you time and simplify your debt-collection processes. They'll have the experience and will circulate regular reminders and provide you with updates on who hasn't paid you.

You already know how important cash is for your

success. That's why it's important to perform regular checks and thorough assessments of your business.

It's also important that you implement the right processes and technology to help improve cash flow - such as improving payment solutions and automated systems.

NON PROFIT ORGANIZATION ACCOUNTING

Certainly, proper accounting is essential for non-trading institutions. These concerns maintain, generally, a cash book and later they prepare a summary of cash transactions appearing in the cash book. This summary takes the form of an account known as receipts and payments account.

Such concerns also prepare 'income and expenditure account' (which is more or less on the lines of profit and loss account) and the Balance Sheet.

The day-to-day accounting consists of maintaining.

- Cash book for recording receipts and payments, and

- Ledger for classification of transactions under proper heads.

Receipts and payments account

It is a summary of cash book for a given period, but the Receipts and Payments account shows the totals of cash transactions under different heads. All the receipts, be cheque or cash are entered on the debit (receipts) side (as in cash book) whereas all the payments (both by cheque or cash) are shown on the credit (payments) side. Following features of the receipts and payments account will help to identify its nature clearly :

- It is not a part of double entry book-keeping. It is just a summary of cash book which is a, part of double entry system.

- Usually, it shows a debit balance which represents cash in hand and at bank. However, in case of bank overdraft, which is larger than cash in hand, the account will show a credit balance.

- Cash and bank items are merged in one column. That means receipts in cash as-well-as by, cheque are entered in one column on debit and payments in cash as-well-as by cheque are entered in one column on credit side. Contra entries between cash and bank get eliminated.

- Both revenue and capital receipts and payments are recorded in this account. For example, ...An organization that is exclusively set up to carryon with the object of carrying out social service or promo & organization of social activities, is a non-trading enterprise. payment for rent and payment for building and machinery both are recorded on its payments side. Similarly, receipts on account of subscription and machinery are shown on the receipts side.

- Just like cash book, it starts with the opening balance of cash and bank and closes with the closing balance of cash and bank.

- It is a summary of cash book, like a cash book, receipts are shown on the debit side and
- payments on the credit side.

- Receipts and payments account fails to disclose gain or loss made by the concern during the period because (a) it is prepared on actual receipt basis i.e. it records all receipts- irrespective of the period to which it relates (previous year, current year or future), (b) it also ignores the nature of the receipts and payments (whether capital or revenue). I

- Accounting concept of gain or loss is based on "accrual concept" which by its very nature "receipts and payments account" is not capable of considering. Therefore, fails to disclose gain or loss (earned or suffered by the concern) during the period. For example, this account ignores:!

  o Decrease or increase i.e. depreciation or appreciation in the value of assets;

  o Increase or decrease in the value of stock;

  o Business charge and appropriation-

whether business expenditure or drawings.

  ○ Provision for expenses incurred but payments not made-outstanding expenses.

  ○ Accounting for payment in advance for the services to be utilized in the next accounting period-prepaid expenses.

  ○ It also fails to distinguish between:

  ○ Capital and revenue payments-whether expenditure or purchase of an asset, and

Limitations of receipts and payments account

Receipts and payments account suffers from following limitations :

- It does not show expenses and incomes on accrual basis.

- It does not show whether the club or society is able to meet its day-to-day expenses out of its incomes.

- It does not show expenses on account of depreciation of assets.

- It does not explain the details about many expenses and incomes. In order to explain such questions, treasurer of the club prepares 'Income and expenditure account' and balance sheet.

Income and expenditure account

This account is prepared by non-trading concerns who want to know if during the financial year their income has been more than their expenditure i.e. profit or vice versa (i.e. loss). Since the object of these concerns is not primarily to' earn profit, therefore, they feel shy in giving it the name of profit and loss account. Because the word 'profit' is a taboo which any society 'looks down upon'. Of course, it discloses whether the concerned institution earned or lost.

It is equivalent to and serves the purpose of 'profit and loss account'.

It is prepared on "accrual basis" (not on receipt basis) meaning thereby that all incomes are to be included which have been earned in the relevant period (whether actually received or not). Similarly, it includes all expenses incurred in the relevant period (whether actually paid or not). This account serves exactly the purpose which 'profit and loss account' serves in a trading concern. On the pattern of 'profit and loss account' income is shown on the credit side and expenditure on the debit side. It also distinguishes between 'capital & revenue' items i.e. it does not take into consideration capital items {both receipts and payments). It follows double entry principles faithfully.

BALANCE SHEET

The balance sheet of a non-trading concern is on usual lines. Liabilities on left hand side and assets on right hand side. In trading concerns, excess of assets over liabilities is called 'capital'. Here, in non-trading concerns, excess of assets over liabilities is called 'capital fund'. The capital fund is built up out of surplus from income and expenditure account.

Distinction between "receipts and payments account" and "Income and expenditure account" :

Receipts and Payments Account

- It ignores outstanding items.
- It ignores credit sales and purchases.
- It includes prepaid items.
- It begins with a balance.
- It is a real account.
- It need not be accompanied by a balance sheet.
- It is like a cash book.
- Closing balance is carried forward to the next period.
- Debit side is for receipts and credit side is for payments.
- Closing balance represents cash in hand and at bank.
- It includes both capital and revenue items.
- It usually shows a debit balance.

- It includes items relating to past, present or future periods.
- It is not a part of double entry system.
- It ignores non-cash items like depreciation, bad debts etc.

Income and Expenditure Account

- It is a nominal account.
- Must be accompanied by a balance sheet.
- It is like a profit & loss account.
- Closing balance is merged into capital fund.
- Debit side is for expenses and credit side for incomes.
- Closing balance represents either surplus or deficiency.
- It includes only revenue items.
- It may show a debit or credit balance.
- It records outstanding items.
- It records credit sales and purchases.
- It excludes prepaid items.
- It does not begin with a balance.
- It includes items relating to current period only.
- It is a part of double entry system.
- It records non-cash items like depreciation, bad debts etc.

Peculiar items of non-trading concern's

Generally, in the exercises, the instructions are given as to the treatment of special items. Such instructions are based on the rules of the concern. These should be followed while solving the question. In cases, where no specific instructions are given, the following guidelines may be considered:

Legacy

It is the amount received by the concern as per the 'will' of the 'donor'. It appears on the receipts side of receipts and payments account. It should not be considered as income but should be treated as capital receipt i.e. credited to capital fund account.

Entrance fees

This is also an item to be found on the receipts side of receipts and payments account. There are arguments that it should be treated as capital receipt because entrance fees is to be paid by every member only once (i.e. when enrolled as memer, hence it is nonrecurring in nature. But another argument is that since members to be enrolled every year and receipt of entrance fees is a regular item, therefore, it should -be credited to income. In the absence of the instructions anyone of the above treatment may be followed but students should append a note justifying their treatment.

Sale of newspapers, periodicals, etc.

As the old newspapers, magazines, and periodicals etc. are to be disposed of every year, the receipts on account of such sale should be treated as income, and therefore, to be credited to income and expenditure account.

Sale of sports material.

Sale of sports material (used) is also a regular feature of the clubs. Sale proceeds should be treated as income, and therefore, to be credited to income and expenditure account.

Subscriptions

The members of the associations, as per rules, are, generally, required to make annual subscription to enable it to serve the purpose for which it was created. It appears on the receipts side of the receipts and payments account and is, usually, credited to income. Care must be exercised to take credit for only those subscriptions which are relevant.

Life membership fees

Generally, the members are required to make the payment in a lump sum only once which enables them to become the members for whole of the life. Life members are not required to pay the annual membership fees. As 'life membership fees' is a substitute for 'annual membership fees', therefore, it is desirable that life membership fees should be credited to a separate fund and fair proportion be credited to income in subsequent years. In the examination question, if there is no instruction as to what proportion be treated as income then whole of it should be treated as capital.

Honorarium

Persons may be invited to deliver lectures or artists may be invited to give their performance by a club (for its members). Any money, paid to invitees, is termed as honorarium and not salary. Such honorarium represents expenditure and will be debited to income and expenditure account.

Specific Donations

These are received for specific purpose. For example: Donation for building; Donation for prizes; Donation for pavilion etc. These are capital receipts and shown on liabilities side. It is worthy to note that such donations should not be treated as income because if they are taken to income and expenditure account, it will increase income. The increased income may be utilized for any other purpose. Thus, the purpose of donation will not be served. Such donations appear on the liability side because they create a long term obligation (liability) on the institution. For example, a donor may wish that prizes may be awarded year after year out of the income earned on his donations. Such a donation account can't be closed within a year by transferring to income and expenditure account.

General donations

These donations are not for any specific purpose and being a recurring income they are to be treated as income and are shown on the income side of income and expenditure account.

Special fund

Legacies and donations may be received for specified purposes. As discussed above, these should be credited to special fund all expenses related to such fund are shown by way of deduction from the respective fund and not as expenditure in income and expenditure account.

Sale of old asset

It is a non-recurring item. It cannot be taken to income and expenditure account. It leads to reduction in asset. Therefore, it is shown by way of deduction from the concerned asset. It is important to note that it is the "book value" that is to be deducted from asset. Profit or loss in such a case is taken to income and expenditure account. Where the book value of asset is nil, the entire proceeds of sale be treated as income.

Endowment fund

It represents donation for a specific purpose. Here, the object of the donor is to provide a source of permanent income to the institution. Thus, it is shown in the liability side of balance sheet. Any income earned during the year in such fund is added to it and any expenditure incurred during the year is deducted from it.

Proceeds of concerts, lectures and dramas or cultural shows

A concert is a program of musical entertainment. Concerts and lectures of eminent personalities are arranged in aid of charitable Accounts of Non-Trading institutions. Amount in the income side of institutions. Amount collected from such shows by sale of tickets is an income of institution and shown in the income side of income and expenditure account.

Accumulated (Capital) Fund

All entities, profit seeking on non-profit seeking require money for carrying out their activities. In business organization such money is called capital while in case of non-profit organizations it is known by various names such as Capital fund or Accumulated fund.

It represents the surplus of assets over outside liabilities of the organization. It is usually made up by special donations; legacies; capitalization of admission fee; life membership fee etc. It is increased (or decreased) by any surplus (or deficit) on the Income and Expenditure account. Some of the lesser known names given to this item are General fund or Surplus account.

Govt. grants. These grants are of two types :

- Maintenance grants; and
- Development grants.

The maintenance grants are for meeting recurring expenses. These are treated as income and shown in the income side of income and expenditure account. The development grant is for acquiring assets. A development grant is a liability.

RECTIFICATION OF ACCOUNTING ERRORS

Accountants prepare trial balance to check the correctness of accounts. If total of debit balances does not agree with the total of credit balances, it is a clear-cut indication that certain errors have been committed while recording the transactions in the books of original entry or subsidiary books. It is our utmost duty to locate these errors and rectify them, only then we should proceed for preparing final accounts. We also know that all types of errors are not revealed by trial balance as some of the errors do not effect the total of trial balance. So these cannot be located with the help of trial balance. An accountant should invest his energy to locate both types of errors and rectify them before preparing trading, profit and loss account and balance sheet. Because if these are prepared before rectification these will not give us the correct result and profit and loss disclosed by them, shall not be the actual profit or loss.

All errors of accounting procedure can be classified as follows:

Errors of Principle

When a transaction is recorded against the fundamental principles of accounting, it is an error of principle. For example, if revenue expenditure is treated as capital expenditure or vice versa.

Clerical Errors

These errors can again be sub-divided as follows:

Errors of omission

When a transaction is either wholly or partially not recorded in the books, it is an error of omission. It may be with regard to omission to enter a transaction in the books of original entry or with regard to omission to post a transaction from the books of original entry to the account concerned in the ledger.

Errors of commission

When an entry is incorrectly recorded either wholly or partially-incorrect posting, calculation, casting or balancing. Some of the errors of commission effect the trial balance whereas others do not. Errors effecting the trial balance can be revealed by preparing a trial balance.

Compensating errors

Sometimes an error is counter-balanced by another error in such a way that it is not disclosed by the trial balance. Such errors are called compensating errors.

From the point of view of rectification of the errors, these can be divided into two groups :

- Errors affecting one account only, and
- Errors affecting two or more accounts.

Errors affecting one account

Errors which affect can be:

- Casting errors;
- Error of posting;
- Carry forward;
- Balancing; and
- Omission from trial balance.

Such errors should, first of all, be located and rectified. These are rectified either with the help of journal entry or by giving an explanatory note in the account concerned.

Rectification

Stages of correction of accounting errors

All types of errors in accounts can be rectified at two stages:

- Before the preparation of the final accounts; and
- After the preparation of final accounts.

Errors rectified within the accounting period

The proper method of correction of an error is to pass journal entry in such a way that it corrects the mistake that has been committed and also gives effect to the entry that should have been passed. But while errors are being rectified before the preparation of final accounts, in certain cases the correction can't be done with the help of journal entry because the errors have been such. Normally, the procedure of rectification, if being done, before the preparation of final accounts is as follows:

- Correction of errors affecting one side of one account Such errors do not let the trial balance agree as they effect only one side of one account so these can't be corrected with the help of journal entry, if correction is required before the preparation of final accounts. So required amount is put on debit or credit side of the concerned account, as the case maybe. For example:

  o Sales book under cast by $500 in the month of January. The error is only in sales account, in order to correct the sales account, we should record on the credit side of sales account 'By under casting of. sales book for the month of January $500".I'Explanation: As sales book was under cast by $500, it means all accounts other than sales account are correct, only credit balance of sales account is less by

$500. So $500 have been credited in sales account.

o Discount allowed to Marshall $50, not posted to discount account. It means that the amount of $50 which should have been debited in discount account has not been debited, so the debit side of discount account has been reduced by the same amount. We should debit $50 in discount account now, which was omitted previously and the discount account shall be corrected.

o Goods sold to X wrongly debited in sales account. This error is effecting only sales account as the amount which should have been posted on the credit side has been wrongly placed on debit side of the same account. For rectifying it, we should put double the amount of transaction on the credit side of sales account by writing "By sales to X wrongly debited previously."

o Amount of $500 paid to Y, not debited to his personal account. This error of effecting the personal account of Y only and its debit side is less by $500 because of omission to post the amount paid. We shall now write on its debit side. "To cash (omitted to be posted) $500.

Correction of errors affecting two sides of two or more accounts

As these errors affect two or more accounts, rectification of such errors, if being done before the preparation of final accounts can often be done with the help of a journal entry. While correcting these errors the amount is debited in one account/accounts whereas similar amount is credited to some other account/accounts.

Correction of errors in next accounting period

As stated earlier, that it is advisable to locate and rectify the errors before preparing the final accounts for the year. But in certain cases when after considerable search, the accountant fails to locate the errors and he is in a hurry to prepare the final accounts, of the business for filing the return for sales tax or income tax purposes, he transfers the amount of difference of trial balance to a newly opened 'Suspense Account'. In the next accounting period, as and when the errors are located these are corrected with reference to suspense account. When all the errors are discovered and rectified the suspense account shall be closed automatically. We should not forget here that only those errors which effect the totals of trial balance can be corrected with the help of suspense account. Those errors which do not effect the trial balance can't be corrected with the help of suspense account. For example, if it is found that debit total of trial balance was less by $500 for the reason that Wilson's account was not debited with $500, the following rectifying entry is required to be passed.

Difference in trial balance

Trial balance is affected by only errors which are rectified with the help of the suspense account. Therefore, in order to calculate the difference in suspense account a table will be prepared. If the suspense account is debited in' the rectification entry the amount will be put on the debit side of the table. On the other hand, if the suspense account is credited, the amount will be put on the credit side of the table. In the end, the balance is calculated and is reversed in the suspense account. If the credit side exceeds, the difference would be put on the debit side of the suspense account. Effect of Errors of Final Accounts

Errors effecting profit and loss account

It is important to note the effect that an en-or shall have on net profit of the firm. One point to remember here is that only those accounts which are transferred to trading and profit and loss account at the time of preparation of final accounts effect the net profit. It means that only mistakes in nominal accounts and goods account will effect the net profit. Error in the these accounts will either increase or decrease the net profit.

How the errors or their rectification effect the profit-following rules are helpful in understanding it :

- If because of an error a nominal account has been given some debit the profit will decrease or losses will increase, and when it is rectified the profits will increase and the losses will decrease. For example, machinery is overhauled for $10,000 but the amount debited to machinery repairs account -this error will reduce the profit. In rectifying entry the amount shall be transferred to machinery account from machinery repairs account, and it will increase the profits.

- If because of an error the amount is omitted from recording on the debit side of a nominal account-it results in increase of profits or decrease in losses. The rectification of this error shall have reverse effect, which means the profit will be reduced and losses will be increased. For example, rent paid to landlord but the amount has been debited to personal account of landlord-it will increase the profit as the expense on rent is reduced. When the error is rectified, we will post the necessary amount in rent account which will increase the expenditure on rent and so profits will be reduced.

- Profit will increase or losses will decrease if a nominal account is wrongly credited. With the rectification of this error, the profits will decrease and losses will increase. For example, investments were sold and the amount was credited to sales account. This error will increase profits (or reduce losses) when the same error is rectified the amount shall be transferred from sales account to investments account due to which sales will be reduced which will result in decrease in profits (or increase in losses).

- Profit will decrease or losses will increase if an account is omitted from posting in the credit side of a nominal or goods account. When the same will be rectified it will increase the profit or reduce the losses. For example, commission received is omitted to be posted to the credit of commission account. This error will decrease profits (or increase losses) as an income is not credited to profit and loss account. When the error will be rectified, it will have reverse effect on profit and loss as an additional income will be credited to profit and loss account so the profit will increase (or the losses will decrease). If due to any error the profit or losses are effected, it will have its effect on capital account also because profits are credited and losses are debited in the capital account and so the capital shall also increase or decrease. As capital is shown on the liabilities side of balance sheet so any error in nominal account will effect balance sheet as well. So we can say that an error in nominal account or goods account effects profit and loss account as well as balance sheet.

Errors effecting balance sheet only

If an error is committed in a real or personal account, it will effect assets, liabilities, debtors or creditors of the firm and as a result it will have its impact on balance sheet alone. Because these items are shown in balance sheet only and balance sheet is prepared after the profit and loss account has been prepared. So if there is any error in cash account, bank account, asset or liability account it will effect only balance sheet.

CONCLUSION

To keep financial accounting of business records from becoming confused with other expenditures made by the business owner, accountants like to use the separate legal entity concept when they are performing financial services for a company, and the personal banking transactions of a person that is small business owner. Some business owners get confused and make withdrawals from their business accounts for personal use, and make the wrong entries in both sets of checkbooks.

Considering basic accounting principles we can determine them as the main rules how the books of any business must be kept and how the financial statements must be prepared. These rules are needed to ensure that it is possible to compare financial statements and accounting information of different businesses and also of the same business for the different periods of time.